FOR THOSE IN PERIL
A history of
Ilfracombe lifeboats

memories
IN PRINT

Editing, design, typesetting: Gudrun Limbrick, Memories in Print

Cover image: ***The Barry & Peggy High Foundation***

ISBN 978-0-9931432-1-2

First published in 2018 by Memories in Print, Woolacombe
www.memoriesinprint.co.uk

All proceeds from the sale of this book go to
the Ilfracombe and District Branch of the RNLI.

The Royal National Lifeboat Institution
supported entirely by voluntary subscriptions

PATRON
Her Majesty the Queen

PRESIDENT
HRH The Duke of Kent

ACKNOWLEDGEMENTS

I am indebted to the staff of Ilfracombe and Braunton museums for their invaluable help; to Rick Tomlinson, Jack Lowe and Andrew Pettey for their permission to use photographs; to all involved with RNLI Ilfracombe for supporting this project; to the records department of the RNLI where the Grahame Farr Archive has been a valuable source of reference; to Frances for proofreading; and finally, our publisher Gudrun Limbrick, for her dedication, skill and patience.

Bob Thompson
Ilfracombe, 2018

We are grateful to Samuels Solicitors for meeting our publishing costs.

Samuels Solicitors, Barnstaple
www.samuels-solicitors.co.uk

Kind donations from the following individuals have covered printing costs:

Brendan Ashford	Yves Clarke
Steve Ashton	Jan Claydon
John Beaman	David Clemence
Mike Beasley	John Clemence
John Bell	Jill Cockram
Martin Bell	Ray Comer
Andrew Bengey	Kevin Cook
Ben Bengey	Cindy Covill
John Blanchard	Rod Donovan
Andy Bradley	Geoff Duffin
Paul Brown	Rob Edwards
Paul Carpenter	Mike Elmer
David Clark	Mark Fay

Adam Fellowes
Geoff Fowler
Peter French
John Fursdon
Peter Gulliford
David Gammon
Mark 'Sparky' Gammon
Bert Gear
Ray Goodman
Leigh Hanks
Graham Heathcote
Derek Hobman
Martyn Hocking
Malcolm Howard
Dave Hutchings
Steve Jackson
Colin Knill
Duncan Laramy
John Lancaster
Roy Lancaster
Tony Maddison
Andy Maslen
Ian Meadlarkin
Marjorie Moore

Polly Morris
Iain Neale
Christine Nelson
Peter Nicholas
John Norman
Matthew Parr
Carl Perrin
Hugo Pettingell
Nick Pedlar
Andrew Putt
Tony Reed
Tony Reeves
Mark Rumson
George Squires
Matt Simpson
Ben Thompson
Frances Thompson
Judith Thompson
Mandy Turner
Dave Turk
Chris Wallis
Clare Wharton-Hobman
Dave Wilson
Ryan Woodger

Donations made in memory of lifeboat supporters:

Beryl Wilkinson by Malcom Wilkinson
Larry Lambell by Andrew Lambell and Michelle Jeffery
Deputy Launching Authority Peter Rawle by Sue Rawle

In memoriam donations for former crew members:

David 'Dinky' Millman by Jean Millman
Robin 'Rumbo' Rumson by Robert Bennellick, Martin 'Mojo' Emburey,
Paul 'Budgie' Hillier and Lee Kift

"The lifeboat drives on with
a mercy which does not quail
in the presence of death;
it drives on as a proof,
a symbol, a testimony,
that man is created in the
image of God, and that valour
and virtue have not perished
in the British race."

Winston Churchill

Contents

A coast with a dangerous reputation

The North Devon coast has been notorious for the dangers it poses to shipping, with consequent loss of life, since the earliest days of maritime trade and travel. At the foot of cliffs rising sheer from the sea, treacherous ridges of rock run out under the surface of the water. The safety of anchorages for ships seeking shelter depends on prevailing winds and tides, and simple instruments for navigation. Under certain conditions, at low tides with strong winds in the northern quarter, there is no safe haven.

Formerly a trading and fishing port, Ilfracombe came to prominence as a holiday resort in the earlier part of Queen Victoria's reign. The harbour was used as a base for Bristol Channel pilots and their cutters (sailing boats) until sixty or seventy years ago. Several places near the harbour have boat-related names, such as Compass Hill, Lantern Hill, and Laston Beach (laston being an old name for a place where vessels discharged or loaded ballast). On Lantern Hill, overlooking the Bristol Channel, is the tiny Chapel of St Nicholas which has been used as a lighthouse since it was built some six hundred years ago. St Nicholas is the patron saint of children, sailors, merchants and pawnbrokers. Other lighthouses in the area were built much later: on Lundy Island in 1820, Hartland Point in 1874, Bull Point in 1877 and Foreland Point in 1900. The Lundy Lighthouse, built on the highest point of the island, was often completely lost in low cloud so was replaced by the North and South Lights in 1897.

St Nicholas' Chapel on Lantern Hill with the light on the left side.
Photograph: Gudrun Limbrick

The birth of a life-saving organisation

Lifeboats had already been established in the United Kingdom before the foundation of the original *National Institution for the Preservation of Life from a Shipwreck* with royal patronage in 1824, renamed the Royal National Lifeboat Institution in 1854. Records indicate that the first lifeboat station was based at Formby, Lancashire in 1777, followed by Bamburgh in Northumberland in 1786.

The Bamburgh lifeboat was a local coble (a type of flat-bottomed fishing boat) converted by a coach-builder, Lionel Lukin, to a design which made it unsinkable. The first completely purpose-built lifeboat, appropriately named *Original*, designed by William Wouldhave and constructed by Henry Greathead, was stationed at North Shields in 1790. One of the earliest lifeboat stations was established at Douglas, Isle of Man in 1802 and most prominent in her crew was Sir William Hillary, who later founded the RNLI.

A memorial to Sir William Hillary, the 'father' of the RNLI, on the Isle of Man. The sculpture depicts a heroic rescue in 1830 during which William himself was washed overboard. Photograph reproduced here with the kind permission of Martin Lloyd.

The RNLI in North Devon

Before the foundation of the RNLI, life-saving facilities already existed in North Devon based on line-carrying rockets. Rockets would be fired which carried a rope into a stricken boat and the crew would be brought to safety on the rope. From 1824 the RNLI provided and funded North Devon's lifeboats as follows:

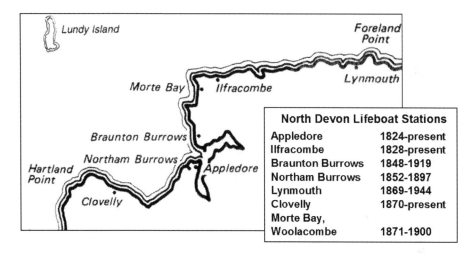

North Devon Lifeboat Stations	
Appledore	1824-present
Ilfracombe	1828-present
Braunton Burrows	1848-1919
Northam Burrows	1852-1897
Lynmouth	1869-1944
Clovelly	1870-present
Morte Bay, Woolacombe	1871-1900

Clovelly's 70ft Clyde class[1] lifeboat *The City of Bristol*, which was permanently crewed, was taken out of service in 1988 and the station closed. The people of Clovelly, however, with typical tenacity, funded and crewed their own lifeboat. This provided valuable service until 1998 when Clovelly once again became an RNLI station.

Early lifeboat launch and recovery (return to dry land) used teams of horses from local farms. This was the case at the lifeboat stations at Braunton and Morte Bay, Woolacombe where the octagonal slats of the carriage wheels stopped them sinking in the soft sand.

---

[1] Lifeboats are grouped into classes which were often named after their designers, eg Watson and Oakley. The names of rivers are now used eg Shannon and Mersey.

The *Robert and Catherine*, Braunton with the team of ten horses used for its launch c1910. Photograph reproduced here with kind permission of the Grahame Farr Archive

Horses pulling back the carriage with its octagonal wheels after the launch of the lifeboat. With thanks to Braunton Museum for the photograph.

The *RNLB (Royal National Life Boat) Violet Armstrong* was stationed at Appledore for 26 years and saved 55 lives She was a 46 foot Watson Class lifeboat with a strengthened hull for crossing the Bideford Bar.

The *Violet Armstrong* (1936 - 1962). Photograph credit: The History of Appledore Lifeboats

The Clyde Class lifeboat *Charles H Barrett* was the thirty-fifth lifeboat provided by the Civil Service Lifeboat Fund and the first of her class of three 70 foot lifeboats. Stationed at Clovelly, she carried a permanent crew of five.

The *Charles H Barrett* (1968-1975). With thanks to David Gammon for this photograph

13

Ilfracombe: harbour of refuge and wrecks

The histories of North Devon include many accounts of disaster and tragedy at sea. Ilfracombe is designated a 'harbour of refuge' which means any vessel in distress can seek shelter within the harbour limits irrespective of its length and there will be no charge of harbour dues. Early records show Ilfracombe has been recognised as a harbour of refuge for more than three hundred years. Sadly, however, some vessels have been wrecked when seeking shelter.

Over the years, large numbers of human bones have been uncovered at Rapparee Cove, to the east of Ilfracombe Harbour. A report of 1856 in the Illustrated London News suggested that bones uncovered at that time at Rapparee could be the remains of Red Hugh O'Donnell and his followers, wrecked as they fled from Ireland during the Flight of the Earls in 1602. The fact that a rapparee was a seventeenth century Irish rebel soldier might add weight to this theory.

The transport *London* was driven ashore at Rapparee Cove in 1796. Two hundred years later, in February 1997, gales and heavy ground seas damaged the cliff-base and retaining wall at the top of the Cove. Sand and rocks were washed away revealing more human bones with pieces of iron. The find was initially linked to the *London*; the media, local and national, reported it as a mass grave of slaves who had drowned, manacled together. Archaeological investigations now indicate that it is unlikely that these particular bones are connected with the *London*. However, there is no question that a large number of people of African origin perished with the *London* and that more than 60 of these had been chained together in the hold of the ship.

Reports vary as to how Ilfracombe's inhabitants reacted to the tragedy of the *London*. According to one account, local people attempted to save those on board, some dying in the attempt. The North Devon Journal, however, reported in 1856 that "...this neighbourhood was guilty [of wrecking] in those days ... and there is a strong tradition that the fate of the *London* was not entirely due to wind and waves."

Ilfracombe's Early Lifeboats
1828: The Pilot Gig

In the early nineteenth century, the local customs collector recommended a lifeboat should be stationed at Ilfracombe. However, as the Commissioners for Customs were in no way responsible for lifeboat provision, this advice was completely disregarded.

A lifeboat was finally established in Ilfracombe in 1828 and the RNLI contributed to the cost of a pilot gig (a large rowing boat) fitted out for life-saving according to the Palmer Plan, a design by George Palmer who was Deputy Chairman of the RNLI. This plan included a system of detachable air cases fitted under the thwarts (the seats), with lifelines and a cork-filled canvas fender around the outside of the boat.

The boat was housed in a building which originally stood in Hiern's Lane. Trafalgar House now stands on the site. The existence of the building is confirmed on an 1852 map of the Harbour. As yet, for this lifeboat and her successor, no records have been discovered.

Pilot gigs can still be seen in the Harbour. Ilfracombe Pilot Gig Club, founded in 2007, still trains in and around the Harbour and competes locally and nationally.

15

1850: The Lady Franklin

A reference to an Ilfracombe lifeboat was made in an 1850 report in the Western Chronicle which examined lifeboat provision in England:

"On the south coast from Dover to Land's End, a distance of 420 miles, there are seven lifeboats, but none at Penzance, where most needed. At the Scilly Isles there is one inefficient boat, the same at St. Ives and Bude, and little better at Padstow. So that from Falmouth round the Land's End, by Trevose Head to Hartland Point, an extent of 150 miles of the most exposed coast in England, there is not really an efficient lifeboat.

"In the Bristol Channel, the North Devon Association maintains three lifeboats in Bideford Bay. There is a new lifeboat at Ilfracombe and one at Burnham. On the south coast of Wales, from Cardiff round to Fishguard, a distance of 200 miles, there is one lifeboat at Swansea and that unserviceable."

The new lifeboat at Ilfracombe referred to is the ***Lady Franklin***. This was a highly sophisticated vessel for her time, ideally suited for her intended purpose. According to local tradition, she was named after the poet, Lady Jane Franklin, wife of the nineteenth century explorer, Sir John Franklin.

The cost of the boat was reported as being £144 which is around £18,200 in today's money. This was, of course, a significant investment and individual donors were asked to contribute to the cost.

The table of these donors on the following page includes a donation of £20 (£2,500 in today's terms) from Lloyds the ship insurers and two shillings and sixpence (around £16) from a 'poor sailor's mother'. It is clear that having a lifeboat was important to a wide range of people.

ILFRACOMBE LIFE-BOAT FUND.
ADDITIONAL SUBSCRIBERS.

	£	s.	d.		£	s.	d.
Mr. Knill Cotton	1	1	0	Mrs. F. Goodwyn	1	1	0
Mrs. Devalaud, Bath	3	0	0	W. Powell, Esq., Lon-			
Capt. Lister	0	10	0	don	0	10	0
Mrs. Thorpe	0	5	0	R. White, Esq., Barum	0	10	0
Mr. Scamp	0	2	0	Capt. May, Broadgate	1	1	0
Capt. Bowden	0	2	0	Mr. Marsh	1	0	0
Mrs. Corbett	0	5	0	Rev. J Blackmore	0	10	0
Poor Sailor's Mother	0	2	6	Mrs. Allan	0	2	0
Mrs. Rouch	0	2	6	Rev. J. D. Ness	1	1	6
Mrs. Thomas	0	5	0	Mrs. Bushley	1	0	0
Capt. Rd. Harding	0	5	0	Messrs. White, Cowes	5	0	0
Mr. Greatman	0	5	0	Mrs. W. Law	2	2	0
Miss Crockford	0	2	6	Miss Amy Chichester	0	10	0
Miss Brownjohn	0	3	0	Cmdr. Hooper, R.N.	1	1	0
Mr. Widlake	0	2	6	Chas. Roberts, Esq	0	10	6
Lloyd's	20	0	0	The Misses Fosse	2	0	0
Rev. P. Johnson	3	0	0	– Guest, Esq	0	10	0
				Mr Nelson	0	5	0

The Committee are anxious to close their accounts for the Purchase and Outfit of the Life Boats, to enable them to lay a statement of their proceedings before the Subscribers at a General Meeting to be convened for that purpose at as early a day as possible, and request that their friends who have not yet paid in their subscriptions will do so at their earliest convenience.

Committee Room, 26th November, 1850

A piece from a local newspaper listing donations made towards the new lifeboat.

A meeting of the Ilfracombe Life Boat Association was held in August 1850 at which it was announced that they had raised enough money to buy a lifeboat. The meeting was then told that the Honorary Secretary of the Association had visited White & Co. in Cowes, a company which had patented and was making a new design of lifeboat. The Honorary Secretary was delighted with what he had seen and the meeting agreed that a new White

& Co. lifeboat should be ordered. The report of the meeting went on to describe the excitement this decision generated:

"The meeting appeared animated by one spirit, and that spirit in the most delightful harmony with the precepts of religion and the dictates of humanity. Following their venerable leader, the whole party drop into their seats, and each pulls with well-timed stroke and vigorous arm his allotted oar – the sure presage of triumphal success. Already with little help of imagination we can fancy the spectators of our future ark utter in Agnes Strickland's[2] lines their excited feelings:

The life boat! The life boat! The whirlwind and rain.
And white crested breakers, oppose in vain,
Her crew are resolved, and her timbers staunch;
She's the vessel of mercy – God speed to her launch!
The life boat! The life boat! How fearless and free,
She winds her bold course o'er the wide rolling sea!
She bounds o'er the surges with gallant disdain!
She has stemm'd them before, and she'll stem them again."

White & Co. built the lifeboat pictured above at the same time as the *Lady Franklin*. The two boats are likely to have looked very similar.

---

[2] Alice Strickland (1796-1874) was a well-known literary historian and poet.

Three months later, the arrival of the new lifeboat was announced in the North Devon Journal:

ILFRACOMBE LIFE BOAT ASSOCIATION
28th November 1850

From unavoidable circumstances we have been unable until now to inform the public of the arrival here, about a fortnight ago, of the splendid boat purchased by this association. This 'Vessel of Mercy' - for the purchase, outfit, and maintenance of which, an Association was formed by the nobility, gentry, and tradesmen of the neighbourhood, aided and supported by Lloyd's Committee, was dispatched from the yard of Messrs. White of Cowes to Southampton, thence to Bristol by rail and thence to this town in tow of the 'Little Western', where she arrived on the 10th inst. under the care of their Hon. Secretary, Mr Huxtable. We are assured that neither care nor expense have been spared to render her as complete in all respects as the skills and ingenuity of her experienced builders could make her. A finer model, we are informed, the momentous service assigned her, cannot well be conceived. She is built of the best Spanish mahogany, well-seasoned by boiling. She is 32 feet long, 8ft beam and three feet deep; double planked - the inner placed diagonally with prepared canvas between; copper fastened; making her completely watertight. She has seven airtight compartments on each side, covered also by double planking fore and aft, and an air tube in both compartments at her stem and stern. A copper water keelson which holds from 7 to 8 [cwt] of water, that acts as ballast, is also for righting her if capsized. She rows 12 oars double-banked with pins and gruminetts if necessary. She has two masts, storm sails, whale-line, grapnel, two life balls, two life buoys, life preservers for the men, and every other requisite; and with the short trial made of her, has proved herself deserving her impressive appellation, a *life* boat. She sails beautifully, throws off the sea she meets without wetting the bow-men, and rides over the water like a sea-bird. It is intended to appoint a day to afford the public an opportunity of witnessing her capabilities, of which due notice will be given.

The ***Lady Franklin*** was replaced after sixteen years. She has no recorded service history.

Days of sail and oar
1866: The Broadwater

"At a meeting of the RNLI, held at the offices, John-street, Adelphi, on Thursday last, it was reported that the committee had ordered the erection of a new lifeboat house at Ilfracombe; also that a new lifeboat was ready to be sent to Ilfracombe – it was the gift of Mr. Robert Broadwater, of Hornsey-rise, in conjunction with his friends, in commemoration of his fiftieth birthday."

Ilfracombe Chronicle, 20th September 1866

Meanwhile, in Ilfracombe a tricky situation was reported in the Western Times of 2nd November 1866:
"On Saturday, a meeting was held at the lifeboat house for the purpose of forming a crew for the new lifeboat, which is shortly expected to arrive in the town. A difficulty was experienced in selecting a coxswain, and after some discussion the meeting adjourned to a future day. The present lifeboat house is not convenient and a building to accommodate the new boat is being erected near the landing pier."

The **Broadwater** was a sailing / rowing, self-righting lifeboat, with ten double-banked oars, and a crew of fourteen plus the coxswain. Photo: Ilfracombe Lifeboat Archives

The Ilfracombe boat house, the committee had decided, was not appropriate for the new lifeboat and so work began to build a new one. While this building has been enlarged from time to time, it housed the Ilfracombe lifeboats right up until the new building was completed in 1996 at the head of the Harbour. The old building now houses Ilfracombe Aquarium.

The photograph below shows the **Broadwater** in the 1866 lifeboat house. The lifeboat was launched using a slipway in front of the boathouse and behind the rocks at Warp House Point. This continued until the old pier was built in 1873. The **Broadwater** and subsequent rowing/sailing lifeboats were then towed by hand along the quay and pulled into the water using the Britannia slipway at the head of the inner harbour.

An 1872 view of Lantern Hill (right) and the 1866 boathouse just to the right of centre. Inset: the **Broadwater** in the boathouse. Photographs are reproduced here with the kind permission of Ilfracombe Museum

21

The first coxswain[3] of the **Broadwater**, from 1866 to 1871, was George Williams. He worked as a boatman for visitors to Ilfracombe. Sadly, George drowned on 26th July 1871 at the age of 40. He had taken a small punt (rowing boat) to look after some bathers in Hele Bay. The tide carried him onto rocks at Beacon Point, near Hele Bay. Two boats set out but were unable to reach him. He was seen struggling in the water and then he went down. His father recovered his body. The Ilfracombe Chronicle reported that *"the deceased was a brave seaman and has been instrumental in saving many lives in connexion with the lifeboat. His good-natured disposition made him a favourite amongst his acquaintances."*

George's funeral was described as *"taking place on the Saturday afternoon with such ceremony and the procession such as perhaps never witnessed in the High Street before"*. George was interred in the cemetery of Holy Trinity Church.

Broadwater Services

By the late nineteenth century, steam tugs were frequently used to tow large sailing vessels to the mouth of the Bristol Channel where they picked up favourable winds. In April 1867, the tow from a tug to the full-rigged ship *Nor'wester* of Boston parted in heavy weather off Morte Point. The wind veered and strengthened into a north-west storm which drove her, dragging her anchors, towards the rocks. The captain's wife and children were lowered by basket into the lifeboat and delivered to Ilfracombe. The **Broadwater** returned to the casualty and stood by all night until the wind eased and a tug was able to take the *Nor'wester* back to Cardiff.

Sailors dreaded being trapped by onshore winds which made it difficult for their vessel to sail clear from the shoreline into open waters. With any onshore wind from the north-west to the north-east, the North Devon coast

---

[3] The coxswain is the person who steers the lifeboat. It is now usually abbreviated to cox.

becomes a dangerous, rocky hazard for sailing vessels. This is known as a 'lee shore'.

The barque *Drago* of Genoa found herself in this dangerous situation on 19th March 1869 when a north-westerly storm brought down her masts. She was found by the coastguard swinging violently at anchor off Morte Stone with her masts cut away. By great fortune, her anchor was holding. This gave the lifeboat at Ilfracombe time to launch (a feat which took three attempts in the heavy, breaking seas) and "pulling lustily, the lifeboat headed westward on its mission of mercy" (according to the Ilfracombe Chronicle). It took four hours to reach the *Drago*.

The lifeboat anchored and struggled to the stricken vessel. Veering, rowing stern first and gradually letting out the rope to the anchor, gave Coxswain George Williams better control of the boat. Still, two oars were broken in the battle against the wind. Sixteen men rapidly slid down a rope into the lifeboat as the wallowing casualty, the *Drago,* threatened to crush the lifeboat against the rocks. The *Broadwater's* anchor was cut away and she was sailed reefed down (which reduces the sail area) into open water where a tug gave them a tow back to Ilfracombe.

The lifeboat crew and sixteen casualties had been drenched by freezing seas during the lengthy, arduous service. All were exhausted but safe. Extra payments were made to the crew for their efforts and bravery in this rescue.

Five years later, the brigantine *Annie Arby* ran a distress signal up a mast and the flag was spotted from Ilfracombe. The *Broadwater* was launched and, with sails set in the strong easterly gale, she overhauled the casualty in Woolacombe Bay under the cliffs of Baggy Point. Crew members chopped away wreckage floating from the *Annie Arby* and she was then taken to a sheltered anchorage.

The *Broadwater* was stationed at Ilfracombe for twenty years and rescued forty-five people. At the end of her service career, she was hauled through the streets of London as part of the pageant at a Lord Mayor's Show.

A lifeboat station at Woolacombe

In 1871, Sir Bruce Chichester gifted land for a lifeboat house close to Woolacombe Beach. The building can still be seen (off the entrance ramp) although it has been much adapted for commercial purposes.

The first lifeboat at Woolacombe was the *Grace Woodbury*. She was 33 feet long and rowed by ten oars. She was replaced in 1892 by the *Theophilus Sydney Echalaz*. Both boats were manned by members of the Ilfracombe crew. The station only had one service in nearly thirty years. This was to the steamer *Lynx* in 1883. The vessel, having sprung a leak off Morte Point, had been deliberately beached by her crew. The *Grace Woodbury* landed her crew the following day when a heavy swell began to build. The *Lynx,* salvaged by the lifeboat crew, was towed to Appledore. The lifeboat station closed in 1900 and the lifeboat transferred to Watchet in Somerset.

The inauguration of Woolacombe's *Grace Woodbury* in 1871.
Photograph courtesy of Ilfracombe Museum

The RNLI has a modern presence at Woolacombe, one of the busiest beaches in the country. RNLI lifeguards are on duty from Easter to the end of the visitor season each year. Working with the lifeguards, Ilfracombe's lifeboats are regularly called to incidents in the area involving surfers and persons missing in the water.

1886: The Co-operator Lifeboats

Record boards on the walls of the lifeboat house show that the Co-operative Wholesale Society of Manchester donated two lifeboats with the same name – *Co-operator No. 2* - to the RNLI, and both were stationed at Ilfracombe. The first of these lifeboats was one of the standard self-righters pulling ten oars. Her first service was to the trawler *Pioneer of Brixham* when her crew was able to save four lives.

The first *Co-operator No. 2* was at Ilfracombe for seven years. She was replaced by the second *Co-operator No. 2* which was longer than her namesake, measuring 37 feet, and had twelve oars instead of ten. It was hoped that this would make her better able to cope with whatever the Bristol Channel had to throw at her.

Brixham fishing trawlers, between 60 and 80 feet long, were powerful vessels specifically designed for speed and towing heavy trawls. At this time, there were 400 in the Brixham fleet making it the largest in the country. These trawlers ranged far and wide from their home port and inevitably some became casualties when pursuing their dangerous trade.

In April 1899, 40 miles west of Lundy Island, one of these Brixham trawlers, *Olive and Mary*, was crippled by huge seas. The damage was extensive: her sails blown out, the bowsprit and boom for the mainsail were smashed, the compass and tender (small rowing boat) had been washed away and waves had stove in the topsides of her hull. Her crew of four chopped away the wreckage and managed to rig a small sail.

They were eventually spotted several miles north of Ilfracombe and *Co-operator No. 2* was launched. The lifeboat, after a first failed attempt in the difficult conditions, managed to tow the *Olive and Mary* to safety.

The crew of the second *Co-operator No. 2* in around 1918.
Photograph reproduced here with the kind permission of Ilfracombe Museum

Five years later, in August 1904, there was a very similar service to the *Bonny Lad of Sennen*, a small fishing boat crewed by a father and son. They decided to run for shelter but failed to avoid the onslaught of a south-westerly gale. Their boat was dismasted and swamped by successive waves. Pumping and bailing out their flooded boat for twelve hours as they drifted helplessly through the night, left them totally exhausted. Rum and biscuits carried by the *Co-operator No. 2* helped them recover from their ordeal. The lifeboat then towed the remains of their boat from Watermouth back to Ilfracombe.

In March 1908, the French schooner *Gracieuse* of Granville, was sighted in distress off Bull Point. The lifeboat was launched to the rescue and, after several hours, returned with the schooner and her crew of five, one of whom, a lad of nineteen, had tragically died from his injuries and exposure. The schooner's stove-in bulwarks (the top sides of the hull, smashed by the heavy seas) and tattered sails were duly repaired and she sailed past Ilfracombe on many subsequent occasions, always acknowledging the kindly treatment received from the local inhabitants by dipping her ensign.

The crew of the lifeboat 1886: WH Barbeary (first coxswain), William Tucker (second coxswain), John Tucker, Richard Souch, Dan Lovering, Richard Lovering (son and father), Charles Buckingham, Thomas Rudd, Roderick Brooks, John Comer, George Comer (brothers), John Bushen, Samuel Ley. Photograph from the Ilfracombe Lifeboat Archive

The Bristol Channel was a hunting ground for U-boats during the First World War. Ignoring the danger, the *Co-operator No. 2*, in her only service of the war, picked up the crew of 33 from the torpedoed steamship *Bengrove* of Liverpool.

In September 1916, *Co-operator No.2* made the twenty-mile voyage to Lundy in only three hours in a full gale of wind. The service return noted that the seas were 'very heavy' and 'feathery white'. This suggests the wind was up to severe gale force 9 and storm force 10. The lifeboat 'filled with water over a hundred times', and the crew, despite protective oilskins were soon 'drenched to the skin'.

Between 1886 and 1921, the two *Co-operator No.2* lifeboats were launched on service 50 times and saved 44 lives.

Problems of launching

Launching lifeboats at Ilfracombe has never been easy. An 1893 report described one particular experiment:

"Co-operator No.2 – Ilfracombe's new lifeboat was severely tested on Tuesday, at the lowest spring tide. Rockets summoned the crew at 1.30pm when it was dead low water, and within half an hour, the boat was launched without the slightest hitch. Tuesday's experiment will prove most valuable, as now, under any adverse circumstances, the boat can be in the water in less than quarter of an hour.

"Before, at dead low water, the greatest difficulties had been experienced in launching the boat, the situation being she had either stuck in the mud, or there being other causes which compelled her to 'stand still', much to the chagrin of the lifeboatmen, and, of course to the utter indignation of the spectators. Mr. William Cole, the honorary secretary to the Ilfracombe Branch of the RNLI, takes upon himself the credit of the new system, and proud he ought to be of the same, seeing how smoothly and successfully it worked upon its first trial. Utilizing the capstan on the Pier for warping

vessels, Mr. Cole persuaded 'headquarters', to send down a Manilla rope and chain, the same being run around a block at the extreme east end of the Pier, and then to the lifeboat, so as to haul her into the water.

"The boat on its carriage was run down on Tuesday from the house to dead low water. The crew, with lifebelts on, then got in her, without entering the water, as was the case on former occasions, and having taken their seats, the hook from the warp was made fast to the chain at the bed of the carriage. The capstan on the Pier was set going with 16 men, one hand spike being broken. The boat was warped with tremendous force until she was out into the water. The carriage would not move at first, but when the rope was attached to the fore bollard of the boat, she was hauled off, and the capstan being set again, she was afloat and clear. The boat then made rapid progress out to sea, standing about four miles off the coast. The weather was very cold, with a strong breeze blowing from the westward, and heavy sea, but the lifeboat behaved splendidly.

"The launching was witnessed by a large number of persons, amongst whom was Captain T. Birmingham, who expressed the opinion that the new plan worked admirably under the most adverse circumstances."

Recovery of the *Co-operator No. 2* on the old Britannia slipway, Pier Road 1918

Survivors from the SS *Bengrove* being brought to Ilfracombe Harbour by the *Co-operator No. 2* in 1915

The second *Co-operator No. 2* on display outside the old boathouse. Photograph courtesy of Ilfracombe Museum

Working on the lifeboats

The crew of the *Co-operator no. 2* probably on exercise in the outer harbour. They are wearing traditional red woollen hats and kapok life jackets[4]. A Bristol Channel pilot cutter can be seen in the background. Photograph courtesy of Ilfracombe Museum

Early records give an interesting picture of conditions and problems experienced in rowing/sailing lifeboats, as well as the harshness of life in a community dependent on the sea. Lifeboats would be sailed to a stricken boat if the winds were from a favourable direction. The sails could be reefed down (reduced in area) in severe weather. When alongside a casualty, the lifeboat would be manoeuvred by oars, requiring fine judgement by the coxswain and skilled teamwork by the crew. Launches were to small fishing vessels caught by sudden changes in the weather or to boats which had run aground in fog. In a particularly poignant case, the lifeboat was not able to save a woman

---

[4] Kapok is a fluffy, fibrous material derived from the seed cases of the tropical kapok tree. It gave both buoyancy and warmth to the life jackets.

who was picking laver[5] on rocks to the east of Combe Martin. She was washed away by the rising tide and drowned. The service return (see page 36) for the attempted rescue reports *"December 3, 1903. Weather very cold with sleet and hail, heavy ground sea".*

Sometimes there were problems communicating with those who were being rescued. On one service return (reproduced on pages 38 and 39) under 'Names of master and owner [of vessel]', the entry simply states "Cannot say. Frenchman".

In the days before radio communications, signal flags were used, but the true extent of a distress could only be assessed when the lifeboat actually arrived on the scene. Communications onshore were relatively efficient owing to the use of telephone and messengers. All coastal villages had coastguards observing the movements of fishing boats. They would be permanently on watch during daylight hours and throughout the night when there was an emergency or when the weather was foul. Lighthouse keepers, who had telephones, were another important source of information.

Launching the lifeboat in these early days had its difficulties, particularly at low tide in the exposed outer harbour. The lifeboat was hauled in and out on ropes, by at least fifty men, many of whom entered the water. In their enthusiasm, they were on one occasion paid the dubious compliment of "taking to the water like rats". During one call-out a gentleman observing the scene had his "trousers ripped from top to bottom" in a launching accident. He was satisfied with a replacement pair "not to cost more than ten shillings" and "two bottles of embrocation" to relieve any bruising!

---

[5] Laver is edible seaweed. This woman was probably trying to feed her family.

The men involved in a call-out were each assigned specific roles so that everyone knew precisely what they had to do.

The **signalman** would follow the lifeboat using coastal tracks, sometimes on horseback, maintaining contact with the lifeboat using flagged signals.

The **launcher** had responsibility for the safe despatch and recovery of the lifeboat. This duty is still required.

Shaftsmen steered the main boat carriage by an articulated fore-carriage.

Watermen pulled the lifeboat into the water, sometimes 'up to their necks', and received an extra 1s 6d for this discomfort.

Blockmen carried wooden chocks to prevent the carriage running away.

Skidmen pulled skids which went under the keel when the lifeboat was being recovered and prevent it becoming embedded in the sand. This duty was required until 1990.

Salvage is a financial claim against a vessel's owners or insurers. It is not in the tradition of lifeboat crews to claim salvage.

Royal National Life-Boat Institution.

LIFE-BOAT *Co. Murator 2.* stationed at *Ilfracombe*

RETURN OF SERVICE on the *3rd* day of *Dec.* 1903

DATE AND CIRCUMSTANCES OF THE CASE.

(If this space is insufficient, please continue the account on the next page, in the blank left for remarks.)

We received a telephone message from the Coastguard at Combmartin saying a woman was drowned on a rock at Sheda Combe 2½ miles E of Combmartin. Having a gale blowing from the WSW Combmartin Road. Launched Life Boat, which was at once launched, and arrived at the spot in all haste, we could do nothing, after woman and we found the life boat could be nothing from the rock by the heavy ground sea before we arrived.

	QUESTIONS.	ANSWERS.
1.	Rig, Name and Port of vessel?	
2.	Names of Master and Owner?	A woman picking laver &c
3.	Number of persons on board?	Surrounded, heavy ground sea
4.	Tonnage; and whether vessel loaded, in ballast, or how occupied, where from and where bound to?	running
5.	Exact position where casualty occurred?	Off Sheda Combe 2½ mile E Combmartin
6.	Nature of casualty, collision, stranding or total wreck?	woman drowned on a Rock
7.	Direction and force of wind? State whether "moderate breeze," "strong breeze," "moderate gale," "strong gale," or "whole gale."	WSW very heavy Gale
8.	Condition of s...	

8. Condition of Sea? State whether "smooth," "moderate," "rough," "heavy," or "very heavy." — *Heavy ground sea*

9. Condition of weather? State whether "fine," "thick," "rain," "snow," "cold," or "very cold." — *Cold, dead thail*

10. Time when signal was first seen or warning received, and state of tide? — *On receiving the warning at 1.50 Pm*

11. Time of Launching Life-Boat? — *tide over five minutes*

12. Time of reaching Wreck? — *Fair wind taking boat till Halfway Point*

13. Time of returning ashore? — *Had to beat place down 6.20 Pm*

14. Time of returning Life Boat to Boat house? — *aft my house after*

15. Number of Lives Saved by the Life Boat? — *None*

16. Number of Lives Lost? — *One woman washed off before we arrive*

17. Was service done under Sails or Oars? — *Both*

18. If under Oars, did Boat pull against wind and sea? — *The Boat pulled splendidly against the wind*

19. How did the Boat behave? — *Splendid*

20. By whose authority was she ordered out? — *The Coxn*

21. Was any Damage done to the Boat? Extent of Repairs required? Are they in hand? — *None*

22. Amount, if any, of Reward received locally or from Gawkers? — *None*

23. Amount, if any, of Salvage? — *None*

Reproduced here is a service return from 1903 when the **Co-operator No. 2** was launched to try to reach a woman washed out by big seas. After each service, a form such as this would be completed to record all the details of the rescue. Tragically, in this case, the woman drowned before the lifeboat could get to her.

Royal National Life-Boat Institution.

LIFE-BOAT *Co-operator No.2* stationed at *Ilfracombe*

RETURN OF SERVICE on the *30th* day of *Nov.* 19*12*.

Date and Circumstances of the Case.

(If this space is insufficient, please continue the account on the next page, in the blank left for remarks.)

QUESTIONS.	ANSWERS.
1. Rig, Name and Port of vessel?	Schooner "Cunicle" of Rumpol. Named for British Ferry Ferry
2. Names of Master and Owner?	Cannot say. Frenchman.
3. Number of persons on board?	five
4. Tonnage, and whether vessel loaded, in ballast, or how occupied, where from and whither bound?	About 200 ton gross
5. Exact position where casualty occurred?	About 10 miles S.E. of Lundy
6. Nature of casualty, collision or stranding. Did vessel become total wreck? If not, state what became of her	Sails nearly all blown away. Gale then was veering and she was bending fresh sails.
7. Direction and force of wind? State whether "moderate breeze," "strong breeze," "moderate gale," "strong gale" or "whole gale".	E. by N. Very heavy gale.
8. Condition of sea? State whether "smooth," "moderate," "rough," "heavy" or "very heavy."	Very heavy sea.
9. Condition of weather? State whether "fine," "thick," "rain," "snow," "cold" or "very cold."	Weather fairly clear very dark
10. Time when signal was first seen or warning received?	About 2.30 a.m. from the Coastguard.
11. Was information of casualty received by telephone or telegraph? If so, attach form containing the message, and those containing any other message.	Telephone from Lundy.
12. Were the adjacent stations informed of the action being taken by the Life-boat?	Yes
13. Time of launching Life-Boat? State of Tide?	About 2 hours. Sent Coasterfor *(See my letter)*

38

14. Time of reaching Wreck? — *About 6 o'clock*
15. Time of returning ashore? — *About 2.30*
16. Time of returning Life-boat to Boat-house? — *About half hour*
17. Number of Lives Saved by the Life-Boat? — *None*
18. Number of Lives Lost? — *None*
19. Was service done under Sails or Oars? — *Sails*
20. How did the Boat behave? — *Splendid*
21. By whose authority was she ordered out? — *Coxswain*
22. Was any Damage done to the Boat? Extent of Repairs required? Are they in hand? — *None. The rest hauled up lashing and was repaired overboard; packed up off the gunwale.*
23. Amount, if any, of Reward received locally or from elsewhere? — *None*
24. Will Salvage be claimed? State amount, if settled. — *None*

NAMES OF CREW	Number of times afloat in the Life-boat on Service.	Special Risk, if any.
1. J. Comer. Coxn.		
2. Lf. Comer. Se. Coxn.		
3. W. Comer. Bowman.		
4. W. Barbeary		
5. M. Williams		
6. J. Lovering		
7.		

NAMES OF CREW	Number of times afloat in the Life-Boat on Service.	Special Risk, if any.
8. Mark Mardella		
9. A. Gillard		
10. W. Irwin		
11. Ben Jones		
12. Tom Irwin		
13. Jack Barbeary		
Geo Irwin		
Le. Ley		

State here the Names of the Crew of the Life-Boat on this occasion, and the number of times they have been off in a Life-Boat to a Wreck; noting (in the third column) any special case of individual exertion.

Signature. (State if on duty) *Jo followed the boat to Happy*

(signed) John Comer — Coxswain-Superintendent.

(Certified) Wm Erle — Honorary Secretary.

Date _____ 196

Service return written in 1912 when a French schooner *Camile* lost its sails in a gale.

John Comer, Coxswain

The Ilfracombe Chronicle, in about 1950, featured an interview with 83 year old John Comer (pictured opposite) who had been coxswain for 28 years at Ilfracombe, and for ten years at Morte Bay. The account describes how he first pulled a lifeboat oar when he was 17 (in about 1884) in the ***Broadwater***. "We used to go out in terrible weather sometimes," he said, "and there were times when it seemed impossible that we should get back to the harbour."

He described a service which lasted seven hours to a Newquay boat, the *Mary Orr* which was in difficulty off Lundy. "On another occasion," John said, "I think the worst gale I remember was blowing at the time, we were called out to a vessel in distress this side of Lundy. We were out from 9pm one day until the following midday when we had to get alongside a pilot boat to get some hot coffee to revive the crew. The cold was intense."

Mr Comer remembered a very busy Ilfracombe of his youth with both inner and outer harbours full and as many as 38 ships coming in on one tide, the smaller vessels replaced in time by the bigger steamships. He also said he was aware there was plenty of smuggling. He told one story of a Spanish galleon going down at Rapparee, and the dead being buried in the cliffs.

Mr Comer saw the disappearance of the small quay cottages and the decline of Ilfracombe as a fishing port. "When I was a young man," he said, "it was possible to make a good living out of fishing but today it is a great struggle. The herring season was then a regular harvest and I have caught as many as 12 to 14 maze[6] at a time. The lowest these were sold for was 12 shillings a maze."

At 83, John was still fishing off his boat *Martha*. He felt that the young lads he saw going about had a soft job. "We used to work hard," he said.

---

[6] There are 620 fish to a maze. The term now seems to be obsolete.

Coxswain John Comer. Photograph from the Ilfracombe Lifeboat Archive.

1921: The Richard Crawley

This 37 foot long lifeboat was built in 1910 for another station and transferred to Ilfracombe in 1921. During the summer months, when the seas are calm and there is no wind, banks of thick fog can roll across the Bristol Channel drastically reducing visibility. On 12th June 1926, in exactly these conditions, a paddle steamer, the *Cambria*, gently ran onto the rocks off Rillage Point, a mile to the east of Ilfracombe.

The **Richard Crawley** raced to the scene and successfully helped fifty of her 500 passengers to safety. Other local fishing and pleasure boats joined the efforts to land the other passengers. The steamer, despite her predicament, had suffered no serious damage and she was refloated on the high tide of that evening.

The Cambria on rocks at Rilledge Point with the *Richard Crawley* alongside.
Photo reproduced here with the kind permission of the Grahame Farr Archive.

The *Richard Crawley* being recovered by manpower in 1930, heading towards the Britannia slipway.

The *Richard Crawley* was the last Ilfracombe lifeboat to be powered by oars and sail.
Photograph courtesy of Ilfracombe Museum

In 1932, the *Richard Crawley* rescued four men who had left their ship in its lifeboats. This turned out to be the ageing lifeboat's final service as there was concern that she was now seriously out of date. Criticisms of her general condition were reported in the Ilfracombe Chronicle. She was sold out of the service, renamed *Hope*, and used as a fire fighting boat during the Second World War.

After lobbying of the RNLI by the Ilfracombe Branch Committee, the provision of the motor lifeboat, *Rosabella,* ended the era of rowing / sailing lifeboats at Ilfracombe.

The Early Motor Lifeboats
1936: The Rosabella

The 32 foot *Rosabella*, built out of a legacy from the late Mr J Hogg of Boscombe, was the first of a new class of lighter 'surf' type lifeboats. She only weighed 3½ tons and was powered, via twin screws, by two 12 horse power Weyburn petrol engines. The *Rosabella* had a speed of seven knots. She carried a crew of seven instead of thirteen.

The *Rosabella* and her crew: (back) Albert Hammett, Raymond Irwin, Les Williams, (front) Tom Williams, George Irwin (second cox), Sid Williams (cox), Bill Barbeary.
Photo from the Ilfracombe Lifeboat Archive

The Ilfracombe Chronicle reported on 13th March 1936:
"Anybody on the quay would have seen Ilfracombe's new motor lifeboat majestically riding the waves, almost at the destination of its journey from

Fremington. When the **Rosabella** *came into the slip a great shout went up from the fishermen and others who had gathered to give it a hearty welcome. The rowing/pulling boat, splendid servant as it has been, was forgotten and everybody's attention was riveted on the spick and span motor boat.*

"A perfect landing was effected on the slip, where the fishermen were waiting to push it out again on the carriage. The fact that many of the helpers were up to their waists in water did not seem to perturb them in the least; they had a job to do and were determined to do it well. Soon the boat was on the water in the harbour again, travelling smoothly and gracefully."

The **Rosabella's** first service was to the ketch *Dido C,* spectacularly and perilously stranded on the rocks at Morte Point in 1936.
Photo reproduced here with the kind permission of the Grahame Farr Archive.

Some of the wartime experiences of the *Rosabella* and her crew, as described in the service returns:

16th January 1940 'At 3.30pm information was received from the coastguard that a large tanker [*the Inverdargle*] was on fire about five miles north of the Foreland. The lifeboat was launched under most exacting conditions at low water with breaking seas driving into the harbour, and a strong, extremely cold north-easterly gale. On reaching the blazing tanker, the lifeboat found a Naval Patrol vessel standing by. The coxswain was informed that there was no one on board the tanker and that no good could be done and the lifeboat accordingly returned'. It was later realised the coxswain had been informed that 'all on board had gone'. Tragically, we can only assume from this message that the remainder of the crew has died.

19th July 1943 'At 9.10pm the Honorary Secretary received a telephone message stating that an aeroplane had crashed off Bull Point and requesting that the lifeboat be dispatched immediately. The lifeboat was launched accordingly and proceeded towards the spot but when about three miles from Ilfracombe met an RAF fast pinnace carrying all five members of the crew of the aeroplane who, with their collapsible dinghy, had been picked up a few minutes before. The lifeboat accordingly returned to Ilfracombe'.

18th October 1944: 'At 2.53pm the Honorary Secretary was informed by NOIC (Navy Officer in Charge) Appledore that an artificial harbour was adrift with crew on board eight miles west-north-west of Morte Point and requested that Ilfracombe lifeboat and crew should stand by ready for service. The lifeboat was taken to the water's edge pending further instructions. Later a message was received that Appledore lifeboat had been launched. Communication was maintained with NOIC and instructions received that Ilfracombe lifeboat was to remain standing by. At 6.25pm an instruction was received that the lifeboat could be returned to boathouse but crew and helpers be available if required. At 10.35pm Appledore lifeboat arrived in Ilfracombe Harbour with seven rescued men and arrangements were made for them to be accommodated for the night.'

The sea conditions for this night were described as 'terrible'. For his perseverance and skilful rescue, Coxswain Sydney Cann, of Appledore, was awarded the RNLI Bronze Medal and the record of thanks inscribed on vellum went to the mechanic/radio operator, John Hooper.

The *Rosabella* was launched 18 times during World War Two, involving long searches in terrible weather conditions which contributed to the frequent requests for the replacement of the rum ration thus continuing the tradition established by the crew of the *Richard Crawley*, whose Honorary Secretary once reported, "the rum was naturally, necessarily consumed". In many respects the war must have been a frustrating period for the Ilfracombe crew as there were 11 launches to aircraft in distress – all with no result. In several cases, the airmen were rescued by neighbouring lifeboats or other vessels.

At the beginning of the war a 47hp caterpillar tractor was supplied, cutting the shore helpers needed for launching from more than 50 men to just 12.

The new caterpillar tractor pictured in 1931 in front of the old boathouse. The tractor made the job of hauling the lifeboat in and out of the water much easier.
Photograph reproduced here with the kind permission of Ilfracombe Museum

During her time at Ilfracombe, the **Rosabella** was launched on service 24 times and saved 12 lives. She was transferred to the Holland Life Saving Society to help repair gaps in their lifeboat fleet resulting from the German occupation. She was based at Terschelling from 1946 until 1955. After being sold out of the service, she fell into disrepair until 2005 when she was restored to her former glory and is now used as an open pleasure boat at Aalsmeer in the Netherlands.

1945: The Richard Silver Oliver

The next lifeboat, of the Liverpool type, was transferred to the Ilfracombe station from Newquay, Cornwall in October 1945. She was the **Richard Silver Oliver** and was to be involved in one of the most distinguished services in the history of the Ilfracombe lifeboats when she went to the aid of the disabled *Monte Gurugu* on 13th November 1949.

A Woolacombe lad, Roy Lancaster, clearly remembers looking out from the Narracott Hotel, across the raging surf and driving spray, and seeing the glow of the burning *Monte Gurugu*. He saw the flash as her boilers exploded. At daybreak, as the coastguards arrived, Roy found a ship's boat on Woolacombe Beach carrying a survivor. It had washed ashore close to the body of a drowned sailor. "It was a sight I have never forgotten," he said. He then momentarily saw the lifeboat in the storm blowing from the north-west, searching along the outer surf line. Roy, as a member of the Ilfracombe Sea Cadets, was in the guard of honour at the funeral service for the lost Spanish sailors.

The following account was given by the skipper of the *Monte Gurugu* to an Ilfracombe Chronicle reporter. *"The terrific force of the sea smashed in the bow plates and the ship began to take water. When it started to settle by the bows, I tried to turn her with the idea of racing for the shore but found the rudder had been broken. She was rapidly sinking and I gave the orders to abandon ship. The water got into her boilers and, as we drew away, she blew up. Previously I had ordered the wireless operator to send out SOS messages which I understand were picked up by the coastguards and transmitted to the lifeboat authority."* Lifeboats were launched from Clovelly, Appledore and Ilfracombe.

At Ilfracombe, the maroons (exploding rockets to summon the crew) were fired at 6.58am and the **Richard Silver Oliver** was launched at 7.18am. The Honorary Secretary's report reads: *"Response to call exceptionally good. Have doubts as to the possibility of boat being able to get outside pier owing to the north-west gale and exceptionally heavy sea. Consulted coxswain, instantaneous request from him to order boat put to sea. Boat heavily swamped before getting past pier and shipped heavy seas past Capstan Point but continued to make headway towards Morte Bay, wind rising and sea much worse. Constant contact kept by radio."*

The Chronicle recorded: *"Through the haze of driving rain and the grey of this tragic November morning, the lifeboat crew espied a speck on the angry seas, and as their lifeboat drew nearer they could see a ship's lifeboat beneath the lofty cliffs of the northern flank of Baggy Point. It was being driven nearer and nearer the breakers."*

In a conversation in 1978, Coxswain George Irwin remembered his crew spotting a ship's lifeboat with 23 survivors under the cliffs of Baggy Point in danger of being smashed onto the rocks. Some of the sailors were struggling with oars to keep her head to sea on the edge of the surf. A grapnel was thrown but missed. It was secured after a second attempt. The boat was pulled clear of immediate danger and the 23 survivors were transferred to the lifeboat.

A cheer went up from the anxious crowd on the pier at Ilfracombe when the **Richard Silver Oliver** messaged at 10.30am: "Landing 23. Ship blew up." The completely exhausted survivors, now suffering from exposure, were landed safely at Ilfracombe and four were immediately sent to hospital. Again from the Ilfracombe Chronicle: "…the little procession provided a piteous spectacle. One man walked bare-footed, and another staggered along in drenched pyjamas. As the men straggled along the jetty, a little woman with tears in her eyes, threw her overcoat around the shoulders of one of them." After re-fuelling and refreshments for the crew, the lifeboat put to sea again in a fruitless search for other survivors. Later in the morning, the Appledore lifeboat landed a lone survivor and five bodies.

Fred Barbeary, a local fisherman, was a crew member for this service and recalled, "It was Nobby Irwin's knowledge and seamanship, particularly in the seas off Morte Point, which saved those men's lives." Fred and other crew members served as bearers at the funerals of the drowned men.

Cox George Irwin was awarded the Silver Medal of the RNLI. Cox Cann of Appledore was given a second Bronze Medal of the RNLI (see page 48 for his first). The three coxes were awarded the Silver Medal of the Spanish Lifeboat Society and a diploma went to all crew members.

Recent correspondence between Bert Gear, a DLA (Deputy Launching Authority), and José, son of the captain of the *Monte Gurugu*, revealed another survivor of the disaster not included in the original statistics – a black cat, Pichirin, belonging to Captain Atela. Pichirin was safely brought ashore in the lifeboat and given to the daughter of the harbourmaster Captain Burfitt. José said his father often mentioned his gratitude for 'the support of the entire town of Ilfracombe'.

In an editorial, the Ilfracombe Chronicle concluded the survivors *"have not been strangers in a strange land. Rather they must have realised that with so much human decency and compassion abroad in this tiny fragment of a sadly disrupted world, there is hope for the future of civilisation"*.

The return of the *Richard Silver Oliver* with 23 survivors from the *Monte Gurugu*
Photograph from the Ilfracombe Lifeboat Archive.

The Ilfracombe Chronicle
18th November 1949

Twenty-five Spanish sailors owe their lives to the tenacity and courage of volunteer lifeboatmen and coast-guards on the Devon coast.

Twenty-three of their number were saved in circumstances which called for the greatest daring on the part of the crew of the Ilfracombe lifeboat.

The captain of the ill-fated vessel, though suffering from the effects of his terrifying ordeal, was quick to praise the superb seamanship displayed by Coxswain George Irwin and the discipline of the crew under his command.

Those with a knowledge of the treacherous seas off this coast were fully aware that the conditions closely resembled those on another occasion when, across the Channel, the Mumbles Lifeboat and her crew were lost in a desperate rescue bid.

Therefore the passage across Morte Bay on Sunday morning was an achievement that must rank high in the annals of the lifeboat service. On shore the generous solicitude shown by the local people for the shipwrecked men was something upon which the town merited congratulations received. Ilfracombe in fact maintained the ancient maritime traditions of Devon – nothing more but nothing less.

1952: The Robert and Phemia Brown

The *Richard Silver Oliver* was replaced by another Liverpool Class lifeboat, the *Robert and Phemia Brown*.

On the 17th January 1954, a vessel was reported in trouble north of Bull Point. The ship turned out to be the Admiralty Tanker *Wave Victor* and it had a serious engine fire. The *Robert and Phemia Brown* was able to get to the boat and rescue ten of her crew, one of whom was injured and was taken to Ilfracombe for treatment.

In her time at Ilfracombe, the *Robert and Phemia Brown* was launched on service fifteen times and saved 23 lives.

The *Robert and Phemia Brown* being launched in Ilfracombe Harbour.
Reproduced here with the kind permission of Ilfracombe Museum.

The *Robert and Phemia Brown* had to be towed to the slipway from the boathouse.
Photographs on this page reproduced with the kind permission of Ilfracombe Museum

It took a team of people to manoeuvre the *Robert and Phemia Brown* onto her trailer.
The cable from her stern goes to a winch on the tractor. On each side of the lifeboat are
balancing poles.

1966: Lloyds II

Lloyds II was the next Ilfracombe lifeboat. This continued the traditional links between the insurance corporation and lifeboat services, established when Lloyds was funding, and providing, lifeboats during the twenty-five years before the foundation of the RNLI (see also the sizeable gift made by Lloyds towards the *Lady Franklin* on page 16). At 37 feet, the Oakley class was the smallest of the RNLI's fleet of off-shore lifeboats.

Richard Oakley had been an apprentice in the boat-building trade on the Isle of Wight and had spent nearly all his working life in the service of the RNLI, being eventually appointed its Naval Architect. His lifeboats were unsinkable because their hulls were divided into eleven water-tight spaces and filled with 180 wooden air cases. Oakley lifeboats would also self-right from a complete capsize in five seconds. This was brought about by 1½ tons of water in a ballast tank below the engine room, taken on as the lifeboat launched, automatically flowing into a righting tank on the port side.

Oakley lifeboats had significant advantages over their predecessors. Twin diesel engines providing 104 hp gave the lifeboat a top speed of over 8 knots. They could carry up to 35 survivors in rough weather and had a range of 182 miles without refuelling. The open wheelhouse shelter of *Lloyds II* was fitted with VHF and MF radio transmitters and receivers. Other items of standard equipment were the echo-sounder, searchlight, loud hailer, and oil spray to smooth rough waters. There were rocket lines which could be used to put ropes aboard a stranded casualty and thus rig a breeches buoy[7] to transfer survivors. Strapped to the stern deck was an emergency tiller for use if the steering system failed, and a drogue (sea anchor) which was towed in heavy following seas to stabilise the lifeboat.

---

[7] A breeches buoy was effectively a large pair of canvas breeches, or shorts, attached to ropes and pulleys between the boat and the shore. A person sat in the shorts and was hauled by coastguards from the stricken ship to safety.

Lloyds II crew 1976: Ian Meadlarkin (assistant mechanic), Dennis Booker (mechanic), David Clemence (cox), John Clemence, Albert Schiller (second cox), Malcolm Joel, Bob Thompson

During 24 years on station at Ilfracombe, *Lloyds II* was gradually modified to keep pace with technological developments in search and rescue. As part of a major refit in 1976, a radar was fitted with a range of twelve miles, and a VHF radio direction-finder which could identify the direction of any casualty transmitting to the lifeboat on an agreed frequency. In a concession to luxury, facilities were provided to make a hot drink.

For many years, there were no spectacular incidents, but routine lifeboat work continued for *Lloyds II* and her crew. The lifeboat was launched in all conditions - from the fairest to the most foul. At various times, disabled yachts were towed to the safety of Ilfracombe and searches were made for people who had fallen from cliffs. In 1973, the long haul to Lundy was made into the teeth of a gale gusting to Force 10. In September 1975, there was a night-long search, close to cliffs and in driving rain, for two boys thought to be cut off on the rocks between Lee and Ilfracombe. The boys were later found sleeping in a public convenience on the outskirts of the town. Some crew members expressed relief that the boys were safe; the comments of the others remain unrecorded!

In 1976, the only service of the year was to the sail-training ship *Winston Churchill* to evacuate a crew member with acute appendicitis. The wind was almost up to gale force and there was a very heavy swell breaking across the *Winston Churchill*. The casualty was lifted aboard at the first attempt and rapidly transferred to an ambulance on the Quay. He was operated on that same evening and made a full recovery.

On 25th April 1981, disaster struck. The owner of the ketch *Spring Tide* attempted to move his vessel to a more sheltered mooring in the harbour. She was bumping against a harbour wall in a swell built up by a severe Force 9 gale, later recorded as gusting to Force 11. The ketch was swept away from the wall and the owner was unable to get aboard. The skipper now in charge decided to put out to sea, presumably to ride out the storm. On board was a boy of twelve and a girl of sixteen. All seemed well although there was no radio contact. Suddenly, at 9.20pm, the *Spring Tide* altered course towards the rocks.

At this point, **Lloyds II** was launched into the gale. She was swamped several times rounding the pier and although close onshore, she disappeared several times in troughs between the huge waves. Also on scene by this time was a rescue helicopter from RAF Chivenor and, within 30 minutes, the girl from the ketch was winched from the water for immediate transfer to hospital. The lifeboat continued the search for the others in appalling conditions until she was recalled from service at 1.40am.

An enquiry later revealed that the *Spring Tide* had been abandoned when a gas leak from a cylinder caused a flash fire. No trace of the boy or skipper was ever found.

For this service, Coxswain David Clemence received a framed letter of appreciation from the RNLI.

Lloyds II launching in a north-easterly gale. Photo: Ilfracombe Lifeboat Archive.

On Sunday 9th September 1984, **Lloyds II** was launched to the yacht *Liberty* which was dragging her anchor close to Rapparee Rocks just beyond the outer harbour. The skipper had died and the only other person on board had no boating experience. In 20 foot waves driven by a north-westerly gale, Coxswain Clemence manoeuvred the lifeboat stern to within feet of the bow of the *Liberty* which was now grounding in the troughs between the waves. The tow was passed and secured to the base of the yacht's mast and she was pulled out of immediate danger. Both vessels were now beam-on to the waves and rolling violently. 200 yards from the outer harbour, the lifeboat twice rolled very heavily to port in the breaking seas. In the relative calm of the outer harbour, a lifeboat crew member was put on board the yacht and sawed through its anchor cable. In the two minutes this took, the weight on the cable had pulled both boats, now lashed together, within 20 yards of Larkstone Rocks. After the cable parted, the *Liberty* was berthed safely against the inner harbour wall. For this service, the Bronze medal of the RNLI was presented to Cox David Clemence. Second Cox Colin Thadwald, mechanic Wayland Smith, assistant mechanic John Fennell and crew members David-Paul Clemence, Andrew Bengey and Maurice Woodger received Medal Service Certificates.

The final service launch of *Lloyds II* was on 20th May 1990 when red flares were reported but nothing found. This completed an Ilfracombe service record of 136 launches and a total of 118 lives saved. This number excludes all those casualties who were helped when in difficult circumstances and whose situation could well have deteriorated without help. *Lloyds II* was eventually transferred to Sherringham in Norfolk.

Lloyds II being taken to the slipway. Photograph by Giampi Alhadeff

Going it alone

Traditionally, the RNLI has rewarded people who have carried out rescues independently of the RNLI. There have been some outstanding acts of bravery by people working on their own initiative. Such rescues are classed as Shore Boat Services by the RNLI.

On the afternoon of 7th June 1975, 14 year old Martin Ruddy, in his 9ft inflatable dinghy off Tunnels Beach, Ilfracombe, noticed a speedboat in distress. Appreciating the predicament of the occupants, he rowed his dinghy for twenty minutes through four foot swells. Martin pulled a man, a boy and a dog aboard his dinghy. A woman whose clothing had been caught in the sinking speedboat was being dragged under for a second time. Martin grabbed hold of her and, with the help of the speedboat owner, managed to release her and pull her aboard. Another man, now numb with the cold of the sea water, was also hauled into the small dinghy. Martin then rowed them all back to the beach through the waves and against the tide.

For his bravery, Martin was awarded the RNLI's bronze medal and an inscribed watch.

Other organisations also reward people who have rescued others in danger. One day in 1918, Ernie Ley, a lifeboat crew member along with his father and brother, saved two boys from rocks. The following day he rescued a man from drowning who had fallen from a paddle steamer. Ernie dived into the sea while still clad in his oilskins and waders to rescue the man.

He was awarded the bronze medal of the Royal Humane Society for his courage and humanity.

Inshore lifeboats (ILBs)

An inshore rescue is one which takes place at sea but close to the shore or from the beach itself. This sort of rescue needs a boat which can easily manoeuvre and get through the surf to reach casualties quickly.

In 1968, Ilfracombe Round Table presented the Ilfracombe station with a three metres long inflatable rubber dinghy which was carried when needed by *Lloyds II* and used for inshore rescues. Over the years it was used to evacuate 30 casualties stranded by the rising tide, including a baby and several dogs. This was not without its risks - one ungrateful King Charles spaniel sank his teeth into the hand of his rescuer.

In one notable rescue on 28th March 1983, seven boys and three adults, some of whom were beginning to show signs of exposure, were lifted using this dinghy from rocks below cliffs at Combe Martin and transferred to *Lloyds II*. For this service, carried out at night and with a falling tide, a letter of thanks was received from the Director of the RNLI.

The *Alec Dykes* inshore lifeboat

After extensive trials in 1991, the D class inshore lifeboat *Alec Dykes* was presented in 1992 to Ilfracombe RNLI by Christine Dykes in memory of her husband. Her estate was also the major contributor to the funding of the ALB (all-weather lifeboat[8]), *Christine and Alec Dykes*, stationed at Brixham in South Devon.

The *Alec Dykes* served at Ilfracombe for nine years responding rapidly to a wide range of emergencies. The *Alec Dykes* remained at Ilfracombe until 2000 during which time she made 125 service launches, which resulted in 52 lives saved.

---

[8] After ILBs were introduced, other lifeboats in the fleet became known as ALBs, all-weather lifeboats. There are operational restrictions on ILBs.

The ILB *Alec Dykes*. Crew Lee Kift (senior helmsman), Robin Rumson and Martin Emburey. Photograph by Rick Tomlinson

Some examples of the casualty situations reported and the results achieved by the *Alec Dykes* and crew:

10th June 1991
Reported casualty: Persons in danger of drowning.
Nothing found by ILB or RAF rescue helicopter.

16th June 1991
Reported casualty: Male, 46, heart attack on board 18ft boat.
Landed to ambulance, then intensive care.

17th July 1992
Reported casualty: Persons cut off by tide, eight children, two adults.
All landed safely, Combe Martin Beach.

15th April 1993
Reported casualty: Person in danger of drowning.
Turned out to be a lobster pot buoy draped with a plastic bag.

21st July 1993
Reported casualty: Two German tourists cut off in exposed position.
Landed at Lynmouth Harbour.

3rd October 1993
Reported casualty: Stranded dolphin.
Gave help to refloat. Animal later died.

5th July 1994
Reported casualty: Person cut off by tide, shock and hypothermia.
Taken to harbour and ambulance.

3rd August 1994
Reported casualty: Person in water – drugs and alcohol.
Put in survival blanket. Stretchered to ambulance.

12th April 1995
Reported casualty: Man and five children (aged 10 to 14). Cut off by tide.
Landed Ilfracombe Harbour.

6th May 1995
Reported casualty: Person having fits on tripper boat.
Given oxygen, landed to care of ambulance.

29th May 1995
Reported casualty: Injured person, with two severed fingers.
Evacuated to ambulance and hospital.

27th December 1995
Reported casualty: Alsatian dog in trouble.
Dog found by coastguard.

27th October 1996
Reported casualty: Vessel adrift, damaged mooring.
Vessel secured.

23rd April 1997
Reported casualty: Capsized canoes, two persons in water.
Survival bags used, transferred to ambulance.

6th July 1997
Reported casualty: Disabled 19ft yacht.
Towed to safety.

11th August 1997
Reported casualty: Person fallen from cliffs, fractured leg and ankle.
Assistance given to helicopter winchman.

The *Alec Dykes* in brief

Known as: ILB or Rubber Duck

Length: 5 metres

Power: 40hp Mariner Outboard

Speed: 20 knots

Crew: Usually three, sometimes two

Response time: Less than 5 minutes

Hazards: Getting into the ILB
                   Getting out of the ILB
                   Bruising when any sea is running
                   Sharp knives
                   Lack of space for sheep

Recipient of the annual award for the most damaged propeller.

August 1991

(quote taken from the service return):

"Telephone call from Swansea Coastguard (CG) that the ILB was required for persons cut off by the tide. Launch agreed. On reaching the casualty it was found that one boy was on a rock in a gulley with two adults in an inflatable dinghy which was punctured, full of water, and a broken 1hp outboard.

"The boy with injured knee and scratches and badly affected by hypothermia, and two adults taken to beach to waiting ambulance … They were all in a nasty situation with some sea running up the gulley."

September 1991 (from the service return)
"SHS[9] paged and on phoning CG requested to launch ON 1165 [station Mersey] following a 999 report of a man in distress in a small craft off Watermouth Harbour. Weather condition SW6. SHS decided to launch ILB as well. ILB reached casualty as ON 1165 was launching. CG requested launch to continue. As ON 1165 came up to casualty, ILB took off the boat's skipper. The CG instructed the ILB to take him to an ambulance in Watermouth. One crew member was put on board the casualty and the craft was towed to Ilfracombe Harbour." The return also recorded: "Mrs Vaughan since informed SHS that but for the prompt services of the lifeboat her husband would be dead."

January 1996
Two brothers, Kirk and Ray Goodman, were fishing at Capstan Point (half a mile to the west of Ilfracombe Harbour) when they were suddenly swept into the wintry sea by a heavy swell breaking over the rocks. Fortunately, the ILB, which should have been withdrawn for winter servicing just two days before, was still available and on the scene within 12 minutes of the call being made. The injured brothers, suffering severely from hypothermia, were given first aid and evacuated to hospital by helicopter from Harbour Beach. As a direct result of this service, there is now an ILB on station at Ilfracombe throughout the year. Relief ILBs are now available when the ILB has to be serviced or repaired.

April 1997
The ILB was called out to two canoeists in trouble approximately two cables offshore (a cable is 200 yards). They were in the water and hanging on to their canoes. Suffering from hypothermia, they were taken onboard the ILB and wrapped in space blankets and survival blankets and brought back to Ilfracombe. The ILB called ahead and ensured an ambulance was waiting for them.

---

[9] The Station Honorary Secretary (SHS) was later to become known as the Lifeboat Operations Manager.

The Deborah Brown inshore lifeboat

Deborah Brown's husband and sons at the naming ceremony of the first boat in her name.
Photograph reproduced with the kind permission of Keith Powell Photography

In January 1996, Deborah Brown, a nurse who devoted her life to caring and helping others, collapsed suddenly having suffered a catastrophic brain haemorrhage. She did not recover and left a husband Paul, and four sons aged from three to eleven. Determined there should be a positive and appropriate outcome to the tragedy they had experienced, the family decided that funding a lifeboat in Deborah's memory would be a fitting tribute. Paul and the boys inspired colleagues and organisations within the Metropolitan Police to support their cause with fundraising events. After 18 months they reached their target of £12,000 and Paul accepted the offer of Ilfracombe as the station to be allocated the ILB. On 4th November 2000, Paul, accompanied by James, Howard, Charles and Daniel, attended the dedication and naming ceremony of the *Deborah Brown* held in the Ilfracombe Lifeboat House. It was a joyous and moving occasion for all those present.

The *Deborah Brown* on a rescue in October 2008. Photo: Ilfracombe Lifeboat Archive

Deborah Brown II Inshore lifeboat

In December 2009, a Bideford fisherman was swept off rocks at Watermouth into rough, cold seas. The waves bowled him over time after time, smashing him into the rocks before the ebb tide washed him out to sea. His wife and other fishermen alerted the coastguard. Amazingly, it was the first time that year he had put on his flotation suit, a garment now commonly worn by anglers both for its warmth and buoyancy qualities. This may have saved his life. Lifeboat helmsman Steve Clemence, using his local tidal knowledge in very lumpy seas and with limited visibility remembers, "We came off a wave, and there he was! Lucky chap."

The next thing the angler knew, the lifeboat was alongside him. By now he was very weak and very cold. He was swiftly hauled on board and taken to Watermouth Harbour to a waiting Coastguard Rescue Team and ambulance. He was taken to the District Hospital suffering from hypothermia and cuts to his head and hands. Four days later, fully recovered, he visited the lifeboat station to thank the ILB crew for saving his life.

The *Deborah Brown II* cutting through the surf with crew members Amy Wigley, Leigh Hanks and Stuart Carpenter. Photograph courtesy of Andrew Pettey.

Significantly, this was the first service for D717 *Deborah Brown II*. Once again, the RNLI and the Ilfracombe Station benefitted from the determination of Paul Brown and his family to support the work of the institution in memory of Deborah. The Metropolitan Police catering organisation, as before, supported their fundraising efforts.

This replacement ILB was an updated development from earlier inshore lifeboats and, as such, was equipped with improved navigational aids and a more powerful outboard which gives an increased top speed of 25 knots.

In another moving naming ceremony, on 28th November 2009, D717 *Deborah Brown II* was launched at Ilfracombe.

ILBs are the inshore workhorses of the RNLI. In Ilfracombe and around the coast, the demands for their services has significantly increased, reflecting the affordability, and availability of a wide variety of ways of going afloat for the public. The approximate average number of services per annum for the *Alec Dykes* was 14 'shouts'. For the first *Deborah Brown* it was 18 per annum and for the second it has been 35 services. Approximately two-thirds of all calls are now answered by ILBs.

Over the years, the majority of calls have been to persons cut off by an incoming tide and follow a typical pattern. Most take place in July and August when visitor numbers are at their highest and awareness of local tidal patterns is at its lowest. Other prerequisites are fine weather and a mid-day low tide which gives access to more remote beaches. Then, by late afternoon or early evening, when potential casualties are probably feeling rather peckish, they realise they are cut off. Mobile phones and waving arms vigorously to passing boats usually raises the alarm. Some of these services can be challenging for the crews particularly when breaking swells surge up a beach or wash over the rocks.

The breakdown of the 46 'shouts' in 2016 includes, six launches to canoes and kayaks; two to jet skis; seven to small boats; one paddle boarder; three dogs; 14 calls to persons cut off by the tide; and other launches which did not result in a service. These are usually made with good intent: malicious false alarms are rare.

On 19th August 2017 a typical service was described in press release issued by the RNLI: "The *Deborah Brown II* was called to aid a kayaker who was in the water at Hele Bay. The sea conditions were exceptionally rough and the casualty had been in the water for almost 30 minutes. The inshore lifeboat crew was quickly on scene, with the all-weather lifeboat on standby. The volunteer crew were able to pick up the kayaker, a man in his 30s with his kayak. On their return passage to Ilfracombe they encountered two to three metre waves, with a rough sea and a large swell. The casualty was brought to the boat house to dry off and given appropriate medical advice."

1990: The Spirit of Derbyshire

In 1983, a programme was begun to introduce fast carriage-launched lifeboats at 22 RNLI stations. As part of this initiative, the Mersey Class lifeboat the *Spirit of Derbyshire* was allocated to Ilfracombe. She was funded not only by an appeal in Derbyshire organised by Winifred Hilton, wife of the Lord Lieutenant but also by Ilfracombe fundraisers who collected in excess of £50,000 towards equipping the lifeboat.

A Mersey Class lifeboat is driven through the water by two V8 turbo-charged Caterpillar diesel engines, each delivering 280 hp. Fitted in the spacious wheelhouse were the latest systems for radio-communications and satellite navigation, along with other important equipment such as VHF direction-finder and first aid essentials. This high-tech machine could take a crew to a casualty dry, warm and in half the time of previous lifeboats.

The *Spirit of Derbyshire* arrived at Ilfracombe on 22nd June 1990. The very next day, she was called out for her first service to a crew member and his fishing boat *Our Fiona Mary* which had broken down near Lundy Island. Two other fishing boats had the casualty in tow but they were struggling against the tide.

There have been some notable services by the *Spirit of Derbyshire*. The first, on 15th August 1990, was to three boats from Combe Martin and Watermouth which had taken visitors out on fishing trips when the wind freshened to a Force 8 westerly gale and the seas became rough. One of the boats, which had fouled its propeller[10], was towed to a sheltered anchorage with two lifeboatmen left on board to assist. Cox David Clemence then took the lifeboat to a second boat, now in Combe Martin harbour where heavy seas were breaking onto the beach making any landing impossible. He turned the lifeboat around in its own length and held her head to sea with skilful use of the engine throttles while a seasick man and boy were quickly transferred to

---

[10] A fouled propeller is one which has become entangled in rope, wire, fishing net and the like preventing it from turning.

the lifeboat. The lifeboat returned to the other boats and eventually fifteen people were landed safely at Ilfracombe. A letter of appreciation was sent from the RNLI's Chief of Operations to Cox David Clemence and his crew in recognition of this excellent service.

The *Spirit of Derbyshire* on the slipway about to launch from the carriage.
Photograph from the Ilfracombe Lifeboat Archive.

On 31st March 1994, according to Cox Bowden of Appledore, conditions on Bideford Bar were the worst experienced for 30 years. The Appledore lifeboat had pulled the fishing boat *Torridge Warrior* clear from the surf, intending to tow the casualty to Ilfracombe. As the seas off Morte Point, to the west of Ilfracombe, were particularly heavy, the *Spirit of Derbyshire* was launched. Between Morte Point and Bull Point, the gale increased to Storm Force 10 and, under the enormous strain, the towing post of the fishing boat came away, destroying its controls. The *Torridge Warrior* was now completely disabled. The Ilfracombe lifeboat took up the tow at 1.30pm, using the fishing boat's stern posts. Eventually, having waited for enough water for safe entry, all three vessels entered Ilfracombe Harbour at 7pm. The Divisional Inspector of Lifeboats, Captain Hugh Fogarty, reported,

"Coxswains Bowden and Putt carried out this service in extreme weather conditions. Both exhibited excellent seamanship." Cox Bowden was awarded the Bronze Medal of the RNLI and Cox Putt received the Thanks of the Institution on Vellum. Other members of the Ilfracombe crew received vellum service certificates.

The Spirit of Derbyshire off Rillage Point. Photograph courtesy of Rick Tomlinson

During the night and in the early hours of 11th November 1995, the yacht *Jakama* got into serious difficulties to the west of Bull Point in very rough seas whipped up by a Force 8 easterly gale. The relief lifeboat *Lifetime Care* was launched at 6.14am. By means of VHF radio-direction finder, she located the stricken yacht which had sustained both sail and engine failure. After several attempts in the severe conditions, Second Cox Andrew Bengey was put aboard the yacht where he found the crew of three in a state of distress. Having ensured their safety, he secured a tow line and the *Jakama* was taken to Appledore and put on a safe estuary mooring. The lifeboat returned to Ilfracombe at 11.08am. For this service, letters of thanks were sent to Cox Andrew Putt and Andrew Bengey.

The Appledore lifeboat *George Gibson* and the **Spirit of Derbyshire** taking part in a medivac[11] exercise with the Lundy supply vessel *MS Oldenburg*. Photo by John Clemence

During her twenty-five years at Ilfracombe, the *Spirit of Derbyshire* was launched on service a total of 343 times. Her work included towing yachts and fishing boats, pumping out flooded vessels, searches at night in all weathers, and operating close inshore or at long range. One casualty was picked up more than 40 miles west of Ilfracombe.

Final records, compiled at RNLI headquarters, show this Ilfracombe lifeboat's services resulted in 460 people being brought to safety.

---

[11] Medivac, or medical evacuation, exercises using volunteers are held to test the responses of the emergency services.

A New Boathouse

Despite huge changes in the design and size of lifeboats and associated equipment, Ilfracombe had been keeping its lifeboats on the same site on the Pier since 1866 when a boathouse was built for the *Broadwater*. It was rebuilt in the same place in 1893 to accommodate the second, and larger, *Co-operator No. 2*. In 1996, 103 years after the *Co-operator No. 2* was first moved into its boathouse, a new boathouse was built on a new site. In a ceremony on 25th May 1996, the new building was opened by Lt. Cdr. Brian Miles, Director of the RNLI. It was funded by Volvo Car UK, the Volvo Dealer's Network, and other voluntary contributions. The site is close to the original boathouse which pre-dated the *Broadwater*'s boathouse.

The new boathouse with *the Barry and Peggy High Foundation* inside.

The spacious new building houses both the all-weather lifeboat and the ILB together with their launch vehicles. It provides dry storage for the crew's protective clothing, their wellies and lifejackets. There is also a meeting room, ablution facilities and a workshop for the mechanics. In 2015, the boathouse was extended to house the larger Shannon class lifeboat.

A new boathouse meant that a new slipway was needed. Before the construction of the new boathouse and slipway, the heavier motor lifeboats were towed along the Quay by tractor, around and past the front of the Royal Britannia Hotel and into the car park. The launchers became expert at bouncing cars onto pavements, and the council at replacing lights damaged when lamp posts were knocked by the lifeboats. From the car park, the lifeboats were pushed past Adele's Café and directly down a slipway. This slipway has since been demolished and replaced with access steps down to Harbour Beach. The new slipway is directly in front of the new boathouse.

The new boathouse and slipway are not the only innovations to make launching easier since the 1990s. Communications have also jumped forward in leaps and bounds. For more than a century, two maroons (rockets) were fired from a mortar tube when the lifeboat was ready to leave the boathouse. They exploded with a booming echo at 600 feet with green and white star shells. The maroons alerted crew members, other harbour users and the casualty, that a launch was in progress. At night they also 'launched' every seagull within miles of the harbour and their screeching cacophony woke the town up. Later on, telephone messages, usually of one word – 'Launch!', were used to call out the crew.

Maroons were fired until the 1990s. There was a brief period of experimenting with modern rockets which exploded at 1,000 feet. With this increased altitude, stations were advised not to fire them if a helicopter was operating in the area. Their unpredictable trajectories were another hazard.

To the relief of neighbours, and after rigorous trials, pagers were phased in. Crew members are now paged (or are alerted by an app on their mobile phones) as soon as a report of a casualty is received, and they immediately drop everything and rush to the boathouse.

2015: The Barry and Peggy High Foundation

The change from an open, 8 knot Oakley lifeboat (*Lloyds II*) with its limited protection, to the Mersey class lifeboat (*Spirit of Derbyshire*) with all the advantages previously outlined, represented a major improvement in SAR (search and rescue) provision at Ilfracombe. Arguably, the arrival of the Shannon class lifeboat was of equal, or even greater significance. The ambition is to replace the Mersey and some Tyne and Trent class lifeboats throughout the RNLI fleet.

The naming ceremony of *The Barry and Peggy High Foundation*. Photo by Tony Gussin

One of most important characteristics of this Shannon class lifeboat is that she can carry 23 passengers and still self-right in rough waters. When the sea is calm, the boat can actually carry a remarkable 80 survivors. Despite her great size (she weighs 18 tonnes), she handles very well and the helmsman can manoeuvre her with ease. She is equipped with excellent radio communications, navigation and radar.

The Barry and Peggy High Foundation has an identification number of 13 – 09 which shows she is 13m in length and is the ninth one built of the Shannon class. Photograph by Gudrun Limbrick

The state of the art tractor and carriage which take the boat to the water mean that the boat can be launched from either the slipway or the beach. The lifeboat is recovered (brought out of the water) bow-first (ie. forwards) on the carriage. The boat is then rotated on its cradle so that she is immediately ready to launch again.

On 26th June 2015, a ceremony was held to mark the re-opening of the extended Ilfracombe Lifeboat Station, and the naming and the dedication of the Shannon class lifeboat. The launch and recovery system for the lifeboat were also named as part of this ceremony. Barry High, OBE, handed over *The Barry and Peggy High Foundation* lifeboat to Paul Boissier, Chief Executive of the RNLI. The foundation donates considerable sums to charitable causes every year. Paul Boissier also accepted from Jon Dillet the launch and recovery system named after June and Gordon Hadfield, whose legacy marked their lifelong support for the RNLI.

Cox Andrew Bengey, who served on the Oakley and Mersey lifeboats (*Lloyds II* and the *Spirit of Derbyshire* respectively), summed up the impact and significance of *The Barry and Peggy High* to the Ilfracombe Lifeboat Station, *"She is an amazing lifesaving asset for our community: faster, safer for the crew and a superb sea boat in heavy weather."*

The 25+ knot speed of *The Barry and Peggy High Foundation* lifeboat, which is the same as the ILB *Deborah Brown II*, gives an improved safety margin for the crews, particularly at night, in rough weather, or when there are several cut off casualties to evacuate. Both lifeboats are now often launched for the same service.

The launch of the ILB is by a Tooltrack vehicle, called the *Denny Booker*, which was recently presented to the Ilfracombe station by Heather Booker in memory of her husband Dennis who was the Station Mechanic on the *Lloyds II*, Oakley-class lifeboat.

After her naming ceremony, *The Barry and Peggy High Foundation* was launched 27 times in 2015. The services included assisting seven vessels with engine failure and giving help to five canoeists. Her service record for 2016 shows calls to six fishing boats, seven yachts/power boats and 12 cut offs. One service involved a passage to Lundy which took only 40 minutes compared to 70 minutes in the *Spirit of Derbyshire*.

A similar pattern of services followed in 2017 which was a quieter year, with no 'shouts' after the recovery of the body of a cliff faller in August until Boxing Day when both boats were launched to search for a missing person, who was later found safe and sound near Woolacombe. The year also ended with the recovery of Bruce the dog, and a coastguard, from a beach near Combe Martin. Bruce had gone over a cliff and was uninjured but stuck on a ledge. The coastguard who was lowered through heavy undergrowth, put Bruce in a dog rescue bag, and they were both lowered to the beach.

Of course, Bruce is by no means the only dog ever to have been rescued by our lifeboats. Oscar, for example, was another grateful customer. On 23rd July 2017, just before 7pm, a call came for help when a dog fell from cliffs on the Woolacombe side of Morte Point.

The Ilfracombe Inshore lifeboat (ILB) *The Deborah Brown II* was launched but, as the weather and sea conditions near the casualty's location were rough, the decision was made to launch the ALB (all weather lifeboat) *The Barry and Peggy High Foundation* to ensure the safety of our ILB crew.

The inshore lifeboat located Oscar, a cocker spaniel, where he had fallen 40 feet from the cliff above. He was valiantly trying to scamper back up the cliff towards his owners, but it was far too steep for him. Two crew went ashore and carried him onto the ILB, then transferred him to the ALB.

Oscar seemed none the worse for his fall and was returned to Ilfracombe lifeboat station where he waited patiently for his owners, who were relieved and grateful for his safe return.

Oscar, second from left, with his rescuers Gillian Cole, Nick Waites and Stuart Carpenter.
Photograph from the Ilfracombe Lifeboat Archive.

Inshore lifeboat Helmsman Stuart Carpenter said *"It was a good call, with a great outcome. The owners promptly called for help and sensibly waited for assistance. If you need help, please do call for assistance rather than endanger yourself."*

Oscar (aged three) said *"I had been enjoying playing in Woolacombe whilst on holiday, but when I slipped my collar, it turned into a 'ruff' day. I am very grateful to my new friends at Ilfracombe RNLI."*

Working with other services

All demands for coastal rescue services, including their own cliff rescue teams and shore patrols, are initiated and co-ordinated by HM Coastguard, on receipt of 999 or other emergency calls. The final decision to launch a lifeboat lies with the Station Operations Manager, a Deputy Launching Authority, and/or the lifeboat coxswain.

In August 1977, a young man was stranded on Hillsborough Beach to the east of the outer harbour. The Coastguard decided to use their 4m GP (general purpose) inflatable for the rescue. The lifeboat was being recovered at the time and assistant mechanic Ian Meadlarkin and Bob Thompson volunteered/were volunteered to crew the GP boat with Dave Taylor of the Coastguard. By this time, the swell had built up and was breaking on the beach boulders. Ian quickly had waves breaking over his shoulders and head. With some persuasion, the casualty got into the GP boat and was landed at the Harbour along with the two bedraggled and saturated lifeboat crew members. For their spirited co-operation with the Coastguard, Ian and Bob were given letters of thanks from the RNLI Director of Operations.

Services have included working with the helicopters of A Flight 22 Squadron RAF stationed at Chivenor, six miles to the south of Ilfracombe. Helicopter winching exercises included firemen as well as crew members of both station lifeboats. Helicopters were initially stationed at Chivenor in 1956, with the sole task of recovering downed aircrew. Civilian emergency missions were secondary to this assigned role but were to become their prime function. SAR (Search and Rescue) flying ended at Chivenor on 5th October 2015. The 'big yellow birds' have been missed by our North Devon community. The responsibility for SAR, under the direction of HM Coastguard, was taken over by Bristow Helicopters based at St Athan in South Wales. The speed and response times of modern helicopters are providing an equally effective service. Helicopters are a major SAR asset, as demonstrated by the ILB rescue of the Goodman brothers on page 67 and the service to the *Spirit of Apricot* on page 88.

Lifeboat People

The old Ilfracombe service returns feature the same family names recurring over the years: Barbeary, Comer, Irwin, Ley, Lovering, Rumson, Williams. Five Comers are recorded on one service return, and five Williams on another. Ted Williams, the first coxswain of **Lloyds II** was the fourth Williams to serve in that position.

Many of the crew members of the rowing/sailing lifeboats are clearly remembered by people in the harbour community. Sam Ley, a local fisherman, recalled in an interview: *"They were hard men. Their lives as fishermen were hard, and going out in the lifeboat, even in the worst of weather was just part of that way of life."*

Another name of note in Ilfracombe lifeboat history is Knill. Charlie Knill gave years of notable service. He was head launcher from 1953 to 1978 and also filled in most other jobs as and when there was a need. Charlie, a milkman, would often abandon his float mid-way through his milk round when the maroons called him to a launch. His customers, well used to this, would collect their own milk from the abandoned float. To his customers' credit, there was never a discrepancy between the milk ordered and the milk that was taken. Charlie's son, Colin, served as the LOM (Lifeboat Operations Manager) from 1985 to 2011.

At the end of 1991, Cox David Clemence, a crew member for whom fishing had been a way of life, retired after 35 years of distinguished service in three successive Ilfracombe lifeboats. Other members of his family also served as crew members on the lifeboats. One of his responsibilities was crew training and he regularly claimed, and still claims, *"I taught 'em all they knewded"*.

David was succeeded by Station Mechanic Andrew Putt who, after 19 years as cox at Ilfracombe, became cox of The Lizard Lifeboat in 2010.

"Ready? Aye ready". Some of the crew in 1918 aboard the *Co-operator No. 2*

Second Cox Andrew Bengey then took over his position, and he is still our cox. Andrew's lifeboat career has followed the traditional route of 'mucking about' in the harbour as a lad (occasionally getting in the way) to working on different fishing boats and tripper boats. As such, he was always around when the lifeboat was launched and recovered. There was a gradual, seamless progression from carrying gear and hauling skids on the beach, to becoming part of the crew. He combined this with a career in accountancy.

At Ilfracombe Lifeboat Station there is a paid staff member and a pool of volunteers. In all, a hundred volunteers are involved in the life of our Station. The crew carry pagers which can go off at any time of day or night, whenever a lifeboat is needed. Crew members then hurry to the lifeboat station ready to face whatever emergency is underway in whatever weather or sea conditions exist.

Lifeboat and shore crew members soon get into the habit of leaving their clothes in a convenient pile so they can dress quickly when pagers go off in the early hours of the morning. There will usually be a brief conversation with partners. Their remarks may or may not be prefixed by 'Darling'. These have been reported to include:

'Turn that pager off'

'Don't worry, I'll make sure the front door is shut'

'Don't catch your big toe in the elastic of your kacks again'

'Don't let the dog out and tell it to stop barking'

'Whose turn is it to look after the kids?'

'Don't wake me up when you get back'

'Be safe'

Coxswain Sydney Williams

Recently a member of the shore crew, after an excellent lunch, was having a Sunday afternoon snooze in a sleeping bag. His pager went off. The sleeping bag zip completely jammed. After a desperate struggle, he did manage to free himself and get to the launch. The sleeping bag, however, was never the same again.

Crew members have no idea what to expect when they are called out, no idea what tragedy might be facing them, the conditions they will have to work in or whether they will be straight back home after a false alarm. Their focus is only on getting the lifeboat in the water and away. The coastguard will then give a 'sitrep' (a situation report) but it is only when the lifeboat arrives 'on scene' that the crew really know what they are facing.

On 20th May 1989, the crew of **Lloyds II** were called out to one of those situations where the full story can only unfold when the lifeboat arrives. The call out was to a capsized catamaran to the north of Combe Martin. There were no further details at that early stage.

The 'catamaran' turned out to be *The Spirit of Apricot*, a 60 feet long ocean racing trimaran, driven by 1,700 square feet of sail on a 90 feet high mast. She had pitchpoled (ie. capsized stern over bow) in lumpy seas and a brisk easterly wind. The helmsman later said, *"we were sailing along and suddenly I was looking down 50 feet at the water below me"*.

When the lifeboat arrived, the crew found the skipper, Tony Bullimore, had already been helicoptered to intensive care at North Devon District Hospital. Two other injured sailors were then lifted from the lifeboat and also flown to hospital. The trimaran helmsman stayed on the lifeboat while there was a search, with the help of a helicopter, for a missing crew member. Tragically, the missing man was never found.

Members of the 2015 crews. Photo reproduced here with the kind permission of Jack Lowe. Jack made this photograph on 12x10 inch glass using Victorian photographic methods as part of The Lifeboat Station Project: lifeboatstationproject.com

By nature, seafarers are a superstitious group of people. Some have a total aversion to any references to small, grey herbivores with fluffy white tails. Blowing air through pursed lips to produce a high-pitched noise is completely forbidden. Some become very anxious in the vicinity of a vicar. Lifeboat crew members have been known to disembark promptly when a vicar has arrived at the boathouse to conduct a ceremony at sea. On one such occasion, the tractor broke down outside the Pier Tavern. The vicar looked most bemused when the coxswain politely enquired if he had also been on the tractor earlier in the day.

In another tradition, rescued casualties often show their appreciation with a contribution to Christmas refreshments. In the past, a casualty donating a single banknote was known as a 'gent', but if there was more than one note the donor was immediately elevated to the status of a 'prapper gent'. These accolades may no longer be used, but gifts are still gratefully received and now, as then, shared with all involved at the station.

Crew members on *The Barry and Peggy High Foundation*. Women have been on operational duties at Ilfracombe for a number of years. Photograph by Gudrun Limbrick.

Ilfracombe's 190-year-old tradition of saving life at sea would not have been possible without the support of our community, its individuals and organisations, also all those who freely give of their time and goodwill. Crucial to our success, and the RNLI in general, are the fundraisers. The RNLI is funded entirely by donations, legacies and fundraising events. It receives no financial support from local or central government. Over the years, fundraising in Ilfracombe has raised many hundreds of thousands of pounds for the cause. The team selling souvenirs has graduated from cardboard boxes and trestle tables outside the old lifeboat house on the Pier to the former pharmacy next to the Royal Britannia Hotel in Broad Street. The shop is staffed on a regular basis by a dedicated team of volunteers.

The Lifeboat Tradition

Lifeboat crews remember the long hours of frustrating searching; the growing realisation that the best of efforts have been in vain; the grim sense of loss. If a search is scaled down, the lifeboat is always quiet on the homeward passage. However, as developments in rescue techniques and technology forge ahead into the twenty-first century, and lifeboats venture further from our shores, more lives will be saved.

Every time the pagers call for a launch, an Ilfracombe lifeboat and its crew will put to sea with hope and determination. It is in this spirit that the service goes on.

The importance of Ilfracombe's lifeboats was best put by Kirk Goodman, who, with his brother Ray, was pulled to safety from the stormy winter seas in January 1996 (see page 67). Kirk remembers, *"When I saw the lifeboat I knew we were safe. I knew we were going to live."*

Our lifeboat crews never know what they are going to face when they set off on a call.
Photograph courtesy of Tony Gussin

A message from our Chair

The vast majority of our RNLI personnel are volunteers. From our brave lifeboat crews who risk their lives to save others, to our generous supporters who make their life-saving possible and all those who work tirelessly behind the scenes. On lifeboats, at lifeboat stations, on beaches, in shops, in schools, at fundraising events, in coastal communities, in museums, in offices, at home or on the factory floor, they all share a common purpose - saving lives at sea.

Could you be part of Ilfracombe RNLI?

For more information on volunteering with us, please call the boathouse on **01271 863771**, or visit our website: **www.ilfracombelifeboat.org.uk**

Thank you for your support.

Jane Perrin
Chair of the Management Committee
Ilfracombe and District Branch of the RNLI

Keep up to date with all our news and events on social media:

 www.facebook.com/IlfracombeRNLI

 @IlfracombeRNLI

 www.instagram.com/ilfracombernli

Services and rescues

The Lifeboats

	Services	Lives saved	Total rescued[12]
Broadwater 1866 - 1886	18	45	
Co-operator no. 2 1886 - 1893	10	4	
Co-operator no. 2 1893 - 1921	40	39	
Richard Crawley 1921 - 1936	10	5	
Rosabella 1936 - 1945	24	12	
Richard Silver Oliver 1945 - 1952	15	23	
Robert and Phemia Brown 1953 - 1966	46	24	
Lloyds II 1966 - 1990	136	118	148
Relief boats	14	23	30
Spirit of Derbyshire 1990 - 2015	343	32	460
Relief boats	34	0	45
The Barry and Peggy High Foundation 2015 - end 2017	65	3	43
Relief boats	3	0	7

---

[12] This figure includes the number of lives saved.

The Inshore Lifeboats (ILBs)

	Services	Lives saved	Total rescued
Trials ILB			
1991	20	9	14
Alec Dykes			
1992-2000	125	52	96
Relief ILB	93	31	75
Deborah Brown			
2000-2009	160	4	155
Relief ILB	89	1	91
Deborah Brown II			
2009 – end 2017	281	15	217
Relief ILB	8	3	13

Two of our decorated coxes. Left, Coxswain Ted Williams, awarded the British Empire Medal for over 20 years' service as coxswain and, right, Coxswain David Clemence of *Lloyds II* who received the Bronze Medal of the RNLI (see opposite page).

Ilfracombe Lifeboat Coxswains

1866 – 1871	George Williams
1871 – 1884	William Barbeary
1888 – 1895	William Williams
1895 – 1923	John Comer
1923 – 1945	Sydney Williams
1945 – 1953	George Irwin ***Silver Medal of the RNLI***
1953 – 1973	Edward Williams ***British Empire Medal for services to the RNLI***
1973 – 1991	David Clemence ***Bronze Medal of the RNLI***
1992 - 2010	Andrew Putt
2010 - present	Andrew Bengey

Over the Wall

The old sailors look over the wall.
And the young sailors too,
once they've learned the right wall to look over
and how to figure wind and cloud and time of day
and flow of tides and currents in the Channel,
moon's seasons, the sea's wrinkles
and how the old mistress can dissemble.
A glance reads her; a lifetime will not fathom her.

The lifeboat sets its course,
point of need sharp in the radar's sweep.
Thumbs-up to the nod from the old men at the wall.
GPS has rendered stars and sun redundant,
but not the old watchers at the wall
with all weathers in their faces.

Frances Thompson